CW01512523

Original title:

Lacy Words Over the Wizard Nail

Copyright © 2025 Swan Charm

Author: Kaido Väinamäe

ISBN HARDBACK: 978-1-80559-293-8

ISBN PAPERBACK: 978-1-80559-792-6

The Ink of Time Woven Beyond Reality

In shadows cast by fleeting light,
Ink drops fall softly, words take flight.
Each moment penned, a tale unfolds,
Stories written in silver and gold.

Eras blend in twilight's grace,
Time's tapestry, a fragile lace.
Woven dreams drift like a sigh,
Echoes linger as stars go by.

Pages turn with whispered breath,
Chasing life, defying death.
Where memories meet the unknown,
In every line, new worlds are sown.

A quill, a muse, a silent pact,
Crafting futures from the past intact.
Moments etched in dusk and dawn,
Each verse a thread, forever drawn.

Through ink and time, we dance and sway,
In woven realms where shadows play.
Each word a journey, a winding road,
The ink of time, a timeless ode.

Celestial Grammar in Ethereal Realms

Stars converse in silent night,
Whispers of joy in cosmic flight.
Galaxies spin with whispered tunes,
Dancing lights, bright as moons.

Syntax of dreams in starlit skies,
Ethereal scripts where hope lies.
Light and dark intertwine and blend,
In these realms, all journeys end.

Nebulas breathe with colors bold,
Tales of the ancients gracefully told.
In this space, our hearts do sing,
Celestial grammar on whispered wing.

Echoes ripple through cosmic seas,
Each moment caught in celestial breeze.
Where time dissolves and shadows gleam,
Reality unfolds, a fleeting dream.

In ethereal realms, we find our way,
Grammar of the stars in bright array.
Connected worlds beyond the light,
Forever dancing in the night.

Intricate Patterns of a Caster's Design

Threads of fate weave in the dark,
Intricate patterns, a hidden spark.
Mysteries dance on the edge of thought,
A caster's design, quietly wrought.

Spells whisper softly, secrets unfold,
In shadows and echoes, stories told.
Woven energy in a silken thread,
Crafted paths where others dread.

Each knot a choice, each twist a fate,
In the loom of time, we contemplate.
Magic flows through every line,
The universe bends as stars align.

Glimmering visions flicker in the night,
Casting shadows, igniting light.
Beyond the veil, where dreams entwine,
The intricate patterns of a design.

With every breath, the magic grows,
Incentive flows where energy goes.
A cosseted world, we find within,
Intricate patterns where dreams begin.

Shadows of Meaning Beneath the Moonlight

In the hush of night's embrace,
Shadows dance with quiet grace.
Whispers weave through silver beams,
Carrying unspoken dreams.

Mysteries lie beneath the glow,
Stories only night can know.
Each flicker a secret shared,
In moonlight's gaze, all are bared.

Rustling leaves and muted sighs,
Echo truths beneath the skies.
The world fades in soft twilight,
Leaving only shadows bright.

As the stars begin to gleam,
Reality blends with our dream.
Each moment, a fleeting grace,
Captured here in this space.

So wander soft beneath the night,
Find the meaning in the light.
For in the dark, we come to see,
What our hearts can truly be.

Bewitched Phrases on Winking Quills

A quill dipped deep in twilight's ink,
Crafting spells with every blink.
Words that swirl like autumn leaves,
In quiet corners, magic weaves.

Sentences that dance and twirl,
Charming thoughts like precious pearls.
Crafted by the hand of fate,
Bewitched phrases resonate.

With each stroke upon the page,
Stories leap from heart to sage.
Winking quills with secrets rife,
Breathing enchantment into life.

In the silence, echoes play,
Painting night and turning day.
Each line a wish, each word a spell,
In this realm, all can dwell.

So take a moment, seek the lore,
In each phrase, adventure's core.
Bewitched by thoughts that softly glide,
On winking quills, let dreams reside.

Threads of Wonder Intertwined with Fantasy

Woven threads of vibrant hue,
Connect the dreams we dare pursue.
In the tapestry of night,
Fantasy blooms, a pure delight.

Each strand a story to unfold,
Whispers of the brave and bold.
In this realm where colors blend,
Imagination has no end.

Twists and turns of fate's own hand,
Guide us to the promised land.
In every twist, a chance to see,
The beauty of our fantasy.

Magic woven into time,
Every heartbeat, every rhyme.
In this fabric, life's embrace,
Infinite dreams find their place.

So let us tread this path anew,
With wonder as our guiding view.
A dance of threads, a bright expanse,
In the world of dreams, we chance.

The Poet's Cauldron of Mystical Tales

In a cauldron, stories brew,
Whispers of the old and new.
Mystical tales with vivid lore,
Awaiting voices to explore.

Stir the pot, let magic rise,
From depths unknown, a world of guise.
Dreams and visions blend as one,
Casting shadows in the sun.

Every tale a spark of light,
Illuminating darkest night.
The poet's heart, a sacred place,
Where every word finds its grace.

In the cauldron's gentle swirl,
Imagination starts to unfurl.
With every drop a spell is cast,
Binding present to the past.

So gather close and hear the rhyme,
For in these tales we freeze the time.
The poet's cauldron holds the key,
To realms of wonder, wild and free.

Treasures Within Obscured Libraries

Amid the dust, the whispers dwell,
Pages hidden, secrets swell.
Ancient tomes with stories spun,
In every word, a world begun.

Spines like shadows, knowledge deep,
Guardians of dreams, in silence keep.
Ink and parchment, time's embrace,
Unearth the magic in this place.

Echoes linger, a gentle hum,
Turning leaves, to wisdom come.
Forgotten verses, lost in time,
Each heart that seeks, a voice will chime.

In the corners, half-lit nooks,
Lie the tales that life forsook.
With each turn, a light anew,
Treasures found in shadows' view.

Journey forth, a quest unbound,
In these tomes, the truth is found.
Each library, a sacred shrine,
Where quiet souls with dreams entwine.

Beyond the Veil: Starlit Poetry

Glistening whispers of cosmic light,
Dance across the velvet night.
Each star a word, a tale to weave,
In the heavens, we dare believe.

Beyond the veil, where shadows play,
Infinite worlds in disarray.
The cosmos sings in silent prose,
As wanderers seek what no one knows.

Nebulas brush like velvet skin,
Filling hearts with dreams within.
A galaxy's sigh, a comet's flight,
The universe pens its starlit rite.

Ink of twilight, brush of dawn,
Crafting verses as we yawn.
In the depths, where wishes lay,
We chase the starlight, night and day.

With every blink, a canvas brushed,
In celestial realms, our spirits hush.
To gather stories, old and new,
Beyond the veil, our essence grew.

Spirals of Imagination Amidst Fading Sigils

In the corners, sigils fade,
Whispers of magic, softly laid.
Imagination spirals wide,
Through the past, we traverse the tide.

Symbols twinkle, secrets spill,
Echoes dance, as shadows thrill.
Winding paths through dust and air,
In fading light, we find our share.

Mystic dreams in ancient runes,
Sway gently like forgotten tunes.
Each swirl a world, a story flowed,
In quiet halls, where wonders glowed.

Chasing echoes of what once was,
Breathing life into the lost buzz.
A tapestry of thoughts untold,
Weaving warmth from threads of gold.

In this spiral, time unwinds,
Unlocking doors within our minds.
Among the sigils, lost but near,
Imagination dances, free of fear.

Threads of Light in the Charmer's Lair

In shadows thick, the charmer waits,
With woven dreams and whispered fates.
Threads of light, in silence spun,
Bewitching hearts, till day is done.

Enchanting tales in flickering glow,
Where every gaze is bound to flow.
Secrets twist like ribbons bright,
Entangled souls in the soft night.

Beneath the surface, a current flows,
Through threads of magic, the charmer knows.
With every glance, a spell is cast,
Binding past and future, vast.

In laughter's echo and soft sigh,
The threads of light will not run dry.
In the lair where wishes bloom,
Hearts entwined in sweet perfume.

Yet beware, for shadows creep,
Holding dreams that gently seep.
In realms of charm, let love take flight,
Through threads of light, we find the light.

Dreamlike Scribes in the Valley of Shadows

In the twilight where whispers dwell,
The scribes pen tales we cannot tell.
Shadows dance with stories untold,
Awakening echoes of dreams of old.

Lost between realms of thought and time,
Their ink flows softly, a mystic rhyme.
Veiled in whispers, secrets arise,
Beneath the watchful, starry skies.

Dreams linger on pages worn thin,
Where fantasies die, and legends begin.
In the valley where night birds sing,
The heart of darkness, the light they bring.

Ephemeral moments in flickering hues,
The scribes weave paths for wanderers' views.
Textures of time entwined, they blend,
In the realm where the dreamers ascend.

As shadows stretch, the night grows deep,
Into the valley, our visions creep.
Silent guardians of the night's embrace,
In this dreamlike world, we find our place.

Enchanted Metaphors in a Wizard's Grasp

In silence, wizards weave their spells,
With words like magic, the air compels.
Each metaphor dances, a shimmering thread,
In the cauldron of thoughts, where dreams are bred.

Wands in hand, they shift the night,
With flicks and whispers, they birth delight.
Stars align in a celestial choir,
As visions ignite like flames in fire.

Ink flows like rivers, secrets unfold,
Crafting tales both daring and bold.
In shadows, the light of wisdom glows,
With every word, the enchantment grows.

Pages turn, revealing the dawn,
In the wizard's grasp, new worlds are drawn.
Through enchanted paths of thought and dream,
They conjure wonders, like a flowing stream.

In the heart of magic, ideas collide,
In the wizard's mind, where mysteries bide.
With every stroke, the canvas ignites,
Metaphors born in the softest of nights.

Arcane Harmonies Blowing Through Ancient Trees

In the forest where giants stand tall,
Arcane harmonies echo, a mystic call.
Leaves whisper secrets in the gentle breeze,
Nature's symphony played through ancient trees.

Each branch sways to a timeless song,
Notes of history where echoes belong.
Hidden in shadows, the melodies play,
Guided by whispers of night and day.

Beneath the boughs, where magic unfolds,
The heart of the forest shares stories of old.
With every gust, the spirits arise,
Dancing in moonlight, beneath darkened skies.

Tangled roots hold the wisdom of years,
Beneath the surface, love and fears.
Harmonies woven from life's embrace,
Nature's breath hums in the sacred space.

In this realm where silence reigns true,
Arcane harmonies invite me and you.
Together we'll listen, together we'll roam,
In the arms of the trees, we find our home.

Syllables of Splendor in a Witch's Brew

Beneath the crescent moon's soft glow,
A witch prepares her potion, slow.
Syllables swirl in the bubbling stew,
A tapestry woven in colors anew.

Her cauldron bubbles with stories untold,
Each ingredient, a memory bold.
Whispers of herbs, spices of night,
In her brew, the stars ignite.

Fingers dance over crystals and stones,
Crafting spells woven of ancient tones.
Syllables echo with power immense,
In the heart of magic, they find their sense.

The air thickens with fragrant delight,
In the shadows, magic takes flight.
Each stirring brings forth the unseen lore,
The witch's brew opens wisdom's door.

In the twilight realm where shadows creep,
Syllables of splendor awaken from sleep.
With every sip, tales of night bloom,
In her brew's embrace, we find our room.

Radiant Rhyme in a Spellcaster's Scroll

In whispers soft, the words align,
A dance of spells, a secret sign.
With crackling light, the runes ignite,
Awakening dreams, in the quiet night.

Ancient tales on parchment lie,
Casting shadows in the sky.
Where magic flows in endless streams,
And every heart can dare to dream.

Through spiral text and luring phrase,
The heart is caught in a mystic maze.
Each verse a portal, drawing near,
To worlds unseen, where hopes appear.

With ink of stars, and fire's breath,
The scroll speaks softly, defying death.
A radiant rhyme that weaves the light,
Binding the fate of day and night.

So journey forth, dear traveler bold,
Seek the wonders the scrolls unfold.
In radiant rhyme, our spirits sing,
Embrace the magic that words can bring.

Illusions Threaded Through the Ink

Ink spills secrets on a page,
Crafting dreams to set the stage.
Illusions dance beneath the quill,
A tapestry of joy and thrill.

Colors swirl in vivid arrays,
While shadows weave in subtle plays.
Each letter bends reality's thread,
Awakening thoughts that linger in the head.

The pen a wand, casting delights,
Filling the day, igniting the nights.
With every stroke, a story grows,
In realms of magic, the ink bestows.

Threads of wonder twine and twist,
In realms where darkness can't resist.
Through illusions' eyes, the truth may shine,
Leaving us lost in the divine.

So let the ink flow free and bold,
With every tale, new dreams unfold.
In illusions woven, hearts may soar,
In the magic of the written lore.

Fantasies Weaved by a Wandering Sage

With cloak of night, the sage will roam,
Through lands unknown, far from home.
Where visions spark like distant stars,
And stories rise from ancient scars.

Whispers of lore dance on the breeze,
As shadows merge among the trees.
With every footstep, a tale he spins,
Of battles lost and quiet wins.

His words, a bridge from heart to heart,
In every pause, a magic start.
Fantasies weave in twilight's glow,
As dreams awaken, set to flow.

Through realms of hope, and depths of fear,
The wandering sage draws ever near.
With wisdom deep and laughter light,
He paints our dreams in shades of night.

So gather 'round, dear friends, take heed,
For every story plants a seed.
In the fantasies we share tonight,
Lives a spark of the endless light.

Shimmering Glyphs Beneath a Starlit Canopy

Beneath the stars, where dreams take flight,
Shimmering glyphs dance with delight.
In the hush of night, secrets unfold,
A tapestry of stories bold.

Constellations whisper tales of old,
Of heroes brave and treasures of gold.
Each glyph a promise, a shimmering guide,
Leading us where the magic hides.

Moonlight paints a path so clear,
Inviting souls that wander near.
In this dance of shadow and light,
We find our truths on the canvas bright.

With every breath, the night grows deep,
As shimmering dreams begin to seep.
Through glyphs of wonder, hearts align,
In the embrace of the divine.

So gaze upon the starlit sky,
Let the magic lift you high.
In shimmering glyphs, we find our way,
Beneath the canopy, we choose to stay.

Whispers of Woven Spells

In shadows deep, the whispers rise,
A dance of dreams beneath the skies.
With starlit threads, the fates entwine,
Each secret murmured, a subtle sign.

Through ancient woods, where echoes dwell,
The heart's desires, the stories tell.
In twilight's glow, the magic stirs,
A tapestry woven, where wonder occurs.

Each silent call, a binding kiss,
In realms unknown, we chase our bliss.
With every breath, a wish is spun,
In the circle of life, we are all one.

Threads of Enchantment in Twilight

Twilight whispers with a sacred sigh,
Softly weaving spells as day says goodbye.
The stars awaken, their secrets to share,
In the loom of dusk, we find magic rare.

Fingers of mist trace stories untold,
As shadows dance and the night unfolds.
Each thread of silver, a promise we bind,
In the fabric of dreams, we're gently aligned.

From vines of moonlight, truth will emerge,
Through the tapestry, our souls converge.
With heartbeats syncing, the night takes flight,
In threads of enchantment, we find our light.

Secrets Breaching the Arcane Veil

From the depths of night, soft secrets seep,
Through the arcane veil, where shadows creep.
In the quiet stillness, the truth unfolds,
A dance of magic in tales retold.

With every heartbeat, the universe sings,
Unlocking the mysteries that silence brings.
The whispers of ancients echo through time,
In shadows we wander, lost in the rhyme.

The veil parts gently, a flicker of light,
Revealing the wonders that dwell out of sight.
Through the fog of doubt, our spirits shall soar,
Embracing the secrets that we can't ignore.

Silken Verses of Magical Craft

In the realm of dreams, where wonders weave,
Silken verses dance, inviting to believe.
With each gentle line, a spell is cast,
A whisper of magic from the future to the past.

Crafted in silence, the words take flight,
Glowing softly in the enveloping night.
As stardust falls, we gather our hopes,
In the tapestry of fate, our spirit copes.

Every stanza a promise, each rhyme a quest,
In this magical craft, we find our rest.
Through pages of wonder, we journey afar,
Silken verses shine like the brightest star.

Melodies of the Arcane in Whispered Rhymes

In shadows deep, secrets sway,
Softly sung, the night gives way.
Flickering lights of the unseen,
Echo through where dreams convene.

Whispers woven in twilight's quilt,
Ancient voices, softly built.
Harmony drifts like leaves in fall,
Enchanting echoes, a siren's call.

Moonlit paths of silver threads,
Glimmers where the magic spreads.
Stars align in graceful tune,
Melodies dance beneath the moon.

With every note, a tale unfolds,
Of daring fates and heroes bold.
Ephemeral as a fleeting sigh,
In whispered rhymes that never die.

Ethereal Notions Adrift in the Spellbound Air

A breeze of thought, so light it glows,
Carried forth where the wild wind blows.
Dreams entwined in gossamer threads,
Whispers trace where starlight spreads.

Suspended high in twilight's arms,
Soft whispers hold a thousand charms.
Wonder swirls in the dusky light,
Filling hearts with pure delight.

Voices rise like mist on dawn,
Ethereal dances from dusk till morn.
Embers of magic softly flare,
In the stillness, truths laid bare.

Lifting spirits, the essence flows,
Beyond the veil where silence grows.
A journey beckons with every breath,
In realms untouched by life or death.

Fragments of Enchantment in the Poet's Grasp

Scattered gems in a garden bright,
Capturing sparks of pure delight.
Ink spills forth, a spell unfurls,
Crafting wonders, as magic swirls.

In the heart of silence, words take flight,
Bridging shadows with beams of light.
Every line, a doorway ajar,
Leading souls to where dreams are.

Fleeting moments caught in rhyme,
Painting echoes of secret time.
With each stroke, the canvas breathes,
Tales of fate spun like autumn leaves.

In twilight's glow, the verses call,
Soft whispers woven, bound for all.
Fragments of beauty, the poet's thread,
Shaping worlds from what is said.

Choreographed Language in a Witch's Dance

Beneath the moon, the shadows wade,
Words like wisps in the night parade.
A dance of syllables, a graceful twirl,
In a mystic realm where spirits swirl.

Each incantation a step to take,
In the rhythm of hearts, the earth will quake.
With every gesture, life ignites,
Ensnaring dreams in spectral lights.

Language flows like a river's bend,
Chasing echoes that never end.
In the space between breaths, they weave,
An artful spell we all believe.

With each motion, the stories rise,
Awakening truths behind disguise.
Choreographed in a witch's trance,
Enchanted worlds in a ghostly dance.

Ethereal Constellations in the Poet's Mind

In the quiet dark they gleam,
Thoughts like stars in a dream.
Twinkling tales of joy and pain,
Whispers dance in silken rain.

Each line a light, a spark divine,
Painting night with vibrant shine.
In the cosmos of my soul,
Inspiration takes its toll.

Galaxies of hope arise,
Tracing patterns through the skies.
Every word a comet's flight,
Guided by the heart's own light.

Through the cosmos, thoughts entwine,
Interstellar, pure, and fine.
Crafting verses, soft and bright,
Euphoria in every write.

Enraptured Cadences in a Sorceress's Heart

In shadows deep, her music flows,
Enchanting whispers, soft and low.
Through moonlit nights, she weaves her spell,
With every note, all longing swells.

Her heart a drum, a rhythmic beat,
In harmony, the world finds heat.
With every strum, the magic blooms,
In twilight's glow, she breaks the glooms.

Melodies rise like mystic smoke,
In the stillness, dreams provoke.
Cadences dance in fervent waves,
Each echo calls, the spirit saves.

Stars align in her embrace,
Every chord a warm, soft place.
Within her songs, the cosmos sings,
Life's enchantment softly clings.

Fantastical Echoes in a Timeless Realm

In a world where moments pause,
Time unravels without cause.
Echos linger, whispered light,
Filling shadows with pure delight.

Through valleys rich and skies so wide,
Imagination is our guide.
Fantastical sights unfold,
Tales of wonder, brave and bold.

Voices of the past resound,
On the air, the dreams are found.
Guided by the winds of fate,
We revel in what's truly great.

Chasing stars beyond the night,
Illuminated, hearts take flight.
In this timeless space, we dare,
To find the magic, everywhere.

Spellbinding Stanzas in the Mystic Fog

Wrapped in fog, the whispers call,
Words cascade, like rain they fall.
In the mist, the dreams entwine,
Textured thoughts, both bold and fine.

From shadows deep, stanzas rise,
Casting spells beneath the skies.
Each phrase a thread, a web we weave,
Capturing what hearts believe.

Illusions dance in soft embrace,
Echoes trace a magical space.
With every line, the world unfolds,
In secret tales, our story holds.

Through the haze, our spirits soar,
Finding treasure evermore.
In the silent, mystic draw,
The verses craft a wondrous law.

Tapestry of Wonders in a Harmonic Flow

In a vale where whispers rise,
Color dances with the skies.
Dreams entwined in golden beams,
Hopes awaken, stir like dreams.

Gentle breezes carry light,
Painting shadows, soft and bright.
Stars align in cosmic tune,
Night unveils a silver moon.

From the earth to heavens wide,
Nature's chorus, side by side.
Melodies of old resound,
Harmony in magic found.

With each thread, the world will weave,
Crafted tales, a heart to cleave.
Voices rise beneath the stars,
Singing dreams from near and far.

In this tale of woven time,
Words and visions intertwine.
A tapestry of heart's design,
In a flow that feels divine.

Haunting Ballads in the Depths of Magic

Down the corridors of night,
Echoed whispers, soft and light.
Shadows dance upon the wall,
Haunting ballads, hear their call.

In the stillness, secrets lie,
Songs of sorrow, spirits sigh.
Casting spells with every note,
In the dark, emotions float.

Through the mist where visions creep,
Melodies awaken sleep.
Ancient tales that softly weave,
Holding hearts, never leave.

In the depths of twilight's grace,
Magic lingers, time and space.
With each chord, a tale unfolds,
In the night, the heart beholds.

Journey forth through starry paths,
Where each echo softly laughs.
In their grip, enchantments fold,
Haunting ballads, stories told.

Phantoms of Syllables from the Abyss

In the void, where shadows play,
Phantoms whisper night and day.
Syllables of ancient lore,
Drift like echoes to the shore.

Words forgotten, lost in time,
Float like whispers, soft and prime.
In the depths, they find their form,
Binding hearts through quiet storm.

Through the silence, spells arise,
Crafted truths, beneath the skies.
With each syllable we find,
Connections woven, soul aligned.

In the abyss, the magic swells,
Carried forth by hidden spells.
Voices merge, a choir's call,
Phantoms rise, enchanting all.

Unraveling the mist of night,
Syllables ignite the light.
In the darkness, we shall see,
Whispers speak of who we'll be.

Threads of Rhyme in the Spellbinder's Hands

With a flick, the fabric blends,
Threads of rhyme, where magic bends.
In the spellbinder's gentle guise,
Woven tales before our eyes.

Colors merge in vibrant dreams,
Dancing lightly, soft moonbeams.
With each word, a rhythm flows,
In the heart, the magic grows.

Stitching moments, time entwined,
Crafting visions, love aligned.
In the tapestry of thought,
Every line is finely wrought.

Poets sing of worlds unwound,
In the silence, beauty found.
Threads of wonder, bright and bold,
In this dance, our tales are told.

Through the weave, a path appears,
Guided forth by hopes and fears.
In the spellbinder's hands, we stand,
Threads of rhyme, a magic strand.

Glimmers of Thought in the Ether's Caress

In stillness blooms a tender light,
Whispers dance upon the air,
Fleeting moments, soft and bright,
Thoughts entwined, a quiet prayer.

Elusive dreams that softly play,
Drift on winds of endless skies,
Glimmers beckon, lead the way,
In the hush, the spirit flies.

Time suspends, the pulse is slow,
Inflections bright, lost in the deep,
Where secrets linger, softly flow,
Cradle visions, dare to leap.

Through the dark, both far and near,
Navigating paths of night,
Kindred souls, we shed our fear,
In the glow of soft starlight.

Awake in shadows, heartbeats roam,
Tales unwritten find their thread,
In the ether, we find home,
Where thoughts linger, ever wed.

Incandescent Echoes of Forgotten Magic

Flickers of a distant song,
Whispers of a world long past,
In the silence, we belong,
Crafted dreams that hold us fast.

Woven through the fabric's grace,
Ink from tales we once believed,
Magic lingers in this space,
In our hearts, it's yet retrieved.

Echoes play like silver streams,
Glances darting, fleeting glow,
In our souls, the ancient dreams,
A forgotten seed to sow.

Through the haze of time and thought,
Glimmers dance with every word,
Holding truths that time forgot,
In the silence, we're unstirred.

From the shadows, stories rise,
In the night, a spark ignites,
In the heart, the magic lies,
Incandescent, it delights.

Mystical Stitches in the Fabric of Night

Tapestry of dreams unfolds,
Stitched with silver, woven gold,
In the dark, a story molds,
Where the night and day behold.

Threads of midnight softly gleam,
Crimson echoes, whispers weave,
Each a tale, a secret dream,
In their embrace, hearts retrieve.

Patterns swirl in cosmic flow,
Guardian stars, ancient light,
Mystical dances, we bestow,
On the canvas of the night.

Embers shimmer, sparkle bright,
In the silence, truths ignite,
With each glance, we set our sight,
On stitches drawn, pure and right.

Awake, we weave what we define,
In the threads of love and time,
Mystical journeys intertwine,
In the dark, our spirits climb.

Silken Sentences from a Timeworn Codex

Pages whisper tales of yore,
Scripted in a glow of grace,
Silken threads, a history sore,
In the ink, we find our place.

Wisdom carved from ancient stone,
In the margins, dreams reside,
Echoes of a world we've known,
Guiding paths where dreams confide.

From the parchment, voices soar,
A melody of evening's call,
Sentences that open doors,
To the depths of heart and hall.

In the shadows, words take flight,
Dancing softly, pure delight,
Through the darkness, they ignite,
Luminous, they paint the night.

Crafted tales with gentle care,
Silken sentences softly gleam,
In our hearts, they form a pair,
Whispering to us, we dream.

Spirited Lines Dancing Over Idyllic Reflections

In twilight's glow, they sway and twine,
Joyful whispers, soft as brine.
They waltz on waves, so wild, so free,
Painting dreams we long to see.

With every turn, the skies alight,
A canvas born of day and night.
Each line a story, bright and bold,
A tapestry of the untold.

Winds of laughter, songs take flight,
Carried by stars, through endless night.
They spin and twirl, in perfect rhyme,
Dancing souls beyond all time.

Reflections ripple on a pond,
Where thoughts arrive, and fears abscond.
With every wave, life's echoes tease,
In harmony with whispered breeze.

Together here, we find our place,
In this embrace, a sweet ballet.
With spirited lines, we rise, we soar,
In idyllic realms we both explore.

Elysian Words in an Unearthly Garden

In gardens lush, where silence sings,
Elysian words take fragile wings.
They flutter near the moonlit blooms,
Enchanted tales amidst the glooms.

Petals drop like secrets shared,
Whispers soft, yet deeply bared.
In every glance, a story flows,
As starlit paths, the garden grows.

Fragrance thick, like dreams retold,
In this realm, our hearts unfold.
A tapestry where shadows play,
In hues of dusk, at end of day.

Rising mist, a veil of grace,
Softly wraps this sacred space.
With every step, we weave our fate,
In this garden, we resonate.

Beyond the boughs, we seek the light,
Elysian words that spark the night.
In whispers soft, the truth is spun,
In an unearthly world, we're one.

Celestial Whispers Captured in Time

Underneath a starry dome,
Celestial whispers find their home.
In timeless echoes, secrets blend,
As night unfolds, and dreams ascend.

Magic flows in patterns bright,
Each twinkling star, a guiding light.
Moments freeze in velvet skies,
Where every hope and wish still lies.

In shadows deep, the cosmos hums,
A symphony of what becomes.
With every breath, we touch the void,
In silence vast, our fears destroyed.

Captured in the still of night,
Whispers shimmer with delight.
Through cosmic realms, our spirits race,
In the heart of time, we find our place.

So hear the call of distant stars,
As dreamers dance 'neath celestial bars.
Together woven in this trance,
In whispers sweet, we take our chance.

Cryptic Notes Beneath a Wizard's Gaze

In candlelight, the shadows creep,
Cryptic notes begin to leap.
A wizard's gaze, both wise and old,
Recites the tales of magic bold.

With parchment crumpled, secrets thrive,
In whispered spells, the world alive.
Each line a riddle, deftly spun,
In the dance of moon, where time is none.

Charmed illusions twist and turn,
As ancient fires glow and burn.
The notes resound, a haunting tune,
Beneath the watchful eye of moon.

In twilight's grip, we feel the weight,
Of dreams that linger, hopes that wait.
With every stroke, the quill does weave,
A wizard's craft we all believe.

So gather near, in mystic thrall,
As cryptic notes enchant us all.
Beneath the gaze of starlit sage,
In whispered magic, we engage.

Creatures of Rhyme Awaken from Silence

In the dark, whispers play,
Echoing dreams in soft ballet.
Shadows dance with rhythmic grace,
Awakening creatures of a hidden place.

Words entwined in velvet night,
Glimmering softly, pure delight.
Fables flutter on gentle wings,
As silence breaks, the heart now sings.

From hidden corners, stories bloom,
Eager hearts dispel the gloom.
Each rhyme a pulse, each beat a spark,
Illuminating a world once dark.

In the still, a chorus grows,
With every line, a river flows.
Creatures chirp from leafy beds,
As poetry dances in their heads.

Awakening joy, a vibrant sound,
Rising high where dreams abound.
Creatures of rhyme, let beauty thrive,
In this universe, we feel alive.

Charmed Words Bound by Affection

In the garden where roses bloom,
Charmed words weave in fragrant gloom.
Tender whispers softly blend,
Each syllable, a love to send.

Bound by threads of warm embrace,
Every glance a sweet trace.
Promises linger, softly spoken,
In this realm, no hearts are broken.

With every laugh, a story grows,
Through open hearts, affection flows.
In gentle tones, we find our way,
Charmed words guide, come what may.

Like fireflies flickering at dusk,
In loving whispers, we trust.
Moments captured in golden light,
Bound by affection, feeling right.

Let your heart join this sweet dance,
In charmed words, we find romance.
Each syllable, a tender sigh,
Together, we'll reach for the sky.

Fragments of Spells in the Celestial Dreamscape

In the hush of starry nights,
Fragments twinkle, soft delights.
Whispers float through moonlit skies,
Spells unspun where magic lies.

Dancing clouds in twilight's hue,
Each breath a wish that feels anew.
Celestial dreams like gossamer thread,
Weaving the paths that we tread.

In this realm of endless grace,
Time uncoils, finds its place.
With every heartbeat, realms collide,
Magic flows like an endless tide.

Fragments held in tender hands,
Floating softly like grains of sand.
Through slumber, whispers take their flight,
In dreamscape realms, we find our light.

Feel the pull of the cosmic seam,
Fragments glimmer in a shared dream.
Together woven, together bound,
In the celestial, our hearts resound.

Fables Flowing From the Cauldron's Heat

In the hearth, the cauldron brews,
Fables rise like morning hues.
Each tale a potion, dark and deep,
Awakening secrets we can keep.

With a dash of faith, a pinch of time,
Every story climbs in rhyme.
Simmering slowly, wisdom gains,
Flowing softly through our veins.

From bubbling depths, enchantments spill,
Tales of courage, dreams to fulfill.
In the heat, we find our way,
Fables guide through night and day.

Echoes linger in the air,
Fables sung with utmost care.
Gather round, let the magic swirl,
In the cauldron, stories unfurl.

As the flames dance, our spirits soar,
Fables flow forevermore.
In every heart, a tale ignites,
From the cauldron's heat, we find our lights.

Fluttering Echoes of Wizardry's Tongue

In shadows cast by candle's light,
Whispers weave through the enchanted night.
Chants of old, a mystic call,
Awakening magic in the hall.

Figures dance in twilight's grace,
With each spell, the air they lace.
Echoes flutter, secrets blend,
In every word, beginnings end.

Potion brews with colors bright,
Stirred with care by hands of might.
Winding paths in dreams they chart,
Crafting wonders, art from heart.

Through a mirror, visions soar,
Mysteries hidden, forevermore.
Sorcery drapes the world in veils,
In fluttering whispers, magic prevails.

Tapestry of Riddles and Fables

In a loom of twilight's thread,
Stories weave on whispers led.
Each tale spun with spice and rhyme,
Capturing hearts in endless time.

Figures dance in patterns rare,
Fables drift in the evening air.
Riddles twine with a clever jest,
In the mind's eye, they find their nest.

Woven colors, bright and bold,
Each narrative, a treasure told.
Layers unfold like petals sweet,
In every stitch, a heartbeat's beat.

Within the tapestry's embrace,
Wisdom glimmers in timeless space.
A dance of thoughts, a playful game,
In riddles lost, yet never same.

Celestial Patterns in Ink and Light

Underneath the starlit dome,
Patterns whisper, call me home.
Ink flows gently, tracing skies,
Drawing dreams from endless sighs.

Galaxies in silver sweep,
Secrets buried in the deep.
Comets flash, a fleeting spark,
In the canvas of the dark.

Planets whirl in cosmic dance,
Inviting souls to take a chance.
Each stroke of light, a tale begun,
In the universe, we are one.

Illuminated thoughts take flight,
Guided by the gentle night.
In the ink of dreams, we write,
Celestial patterns, bold and bright.

The Enchanter's Artful Cadence

With a flick of wrist, the magic glows,
In rhythm with the heart that knows.
Notes of wonder dance in air,
Enchantment stirs with utmost care.

Fingers weave through whispered spells,
In every tone, a story dwells.
Breath of life in every word,
As melodies of dreams are heard.

Harmony sings through twilight's veil,
Echoing soft, like a distant trail.
Cadence binds the world in thrall,
An enchanter's art, a siren's call.

Songs of ages swirl like mist,
In skimming light, the shadows kissed.
Crafting moments, fleeting, rare,
In every note, we find despair.

Gossamer Threads of Whispered Charms

In twilight's gentle, woven light,
A tapestry of dreams takes flight.
Whispers dance on the evening air,
Threads of hope, delicate and rare.

Moonlit smiles paint the sky's embrace,
With every heartbeat, the stars interlace.
Soft secrets float on a breeze so sweet,
In the hush of night, our spirits meet.

Glimmers of magic in shadows play,
As wishes drift like leaves in May.
Charmed moments caught in the silver glow,
Where the heart learns what it long to know.

Ethereal echoes whispering low,
In the garden of dreams, we softly sow.
A symphony of sighs, a gentle mist,
In every heartbeat, a tender tryst.

Awake we linger, in starlit streams,
Together merging our silent dreams.
The world fades away, just you and I,
With gossamer threads, we learn to fly.

Charmed Quatrains Beneath the Stars

Beneath the stars, our dreams collide,
In whispered wishes, we confide.
Galaxies spin, tales intertwine,
In every heartbeat, our souls define.

Crickets sing a sonnet in the night,
As lanterns glow with soft, warm light.
The cosmos hums an ancient tune,
And shadows dance beneath the moon.

Each star a promise, bright and bold,
In silvered skies, our hopes unfold.
Every twinkle a memory dear,
In the quiet dark, you draw me near.

With you I wander through twilight's veil,
In the glow of stories, we set sail.
Charmed by starlight, our spirits fly,
In this cosmic tapestry, we lie.

The universe whispers secrets untold,
In the chilly night, the warmth we hold.
Together we wander, hearts in sync,
In a dance of stars, we find our link.

Mirrored Reflections of Arcane Poetry

In mirrors of silver, the past appears,
Echoes of laughter, shadows of fears.
Reflections twist in twilight's glow,
A dance of memories, ebb and flow.

Each glimpse a riddle, wrapped in time,
Where ancient verses twist and rhyme.
In whispered tones, the truth unfurls,
Arcane secrets from other worlds.

Pages flutter like wings of night,
Illuminated by soft starlight.
In the realm of dreams, we weave our tale,
With every breath, our hopes prevail.

Mysteries linger in the sacred space,
In the mirror's gaze, I trace your face.
Hands outstretched toward infinity,
We capture the essence of what will be.

In silent supplication, hearts abide,
For every reflection holds a guide.
Together we wander these mirrored halls,
In the dance of life, true beauty calls.

Starlit Stanzas in a Forgotten Language

In starlit shadows, verses unfold,
A forgotten tongue, a story told.
The night speaks softly, without a sound,
In ancient whispers, wisdom found.

Constellations weave a tapestry bright,
Guided by dreams that take flight.
With each line, the cosmos sighs,
In the depths of night, our spirits rise.

Echoes of passion in the midnight air,
Stanzas of longing, a delicate dare.
We're lost in realms where time stands still,
With every heartbeat, we chase our will.

The ink of stars flows through the dark,
Painting our souls with every spark.
We gather the stories from ages past,
In the language of light, forever cast.

As dawn approaches, we hold the dream,
In every heartbeat, a vibrant theme.
Starlit stanzas, a gentle balm,
In the presence of magic, we find our calm.

Inked Charms in a Dreamweaver's Spellbook

In the pages of night, secrets unfurl,
Whispers of dreams in each delicate swirl.
Inked charms awaken, the slumbering art,
Guided by moonbeams that dance in the heart.

Ephemeral visions in twilight's embrace,
Crafted with care, each line finds its place.
A tapestry woven of shadows and light,
Breathless enchantments that bloom in the night.

Spells echo softly in stillness profound,
Plucking at heartstrings, a symphonic sound.
Each word a beacon that pierces the gloom,
An invitation to wander, and freely consume.

Circles and spirals, the ink takes to flight,
Sparkling with magic, igniting the night.
A dreamweaver's gift, a promise sublime,
Inked charms whispering tales out of time.

In a world where shadows and wishes entwine,
In every soft sigh, the magic is mine.
Holding the spellbook with reverent hands,
Inked charms of the dreamer, where wonder expands.

Shadows Cast by a Truthful Spellbook

In a library dim, the spellbook lies bare,
Shadows gather thick, weaving tales of despair.
Each page a reflection of honesty's might,
Echoing truths that unfold in the night.

Silhouettes dance in the flickering light,
Casting shadows that lurch, twist, and bite.
Words etched in ink, their honesty shines,
Revealing the secrets that destiny binds.

Beneath the cloak of the candle's soft glow,
Lies the weight of the stories that only few know.
In their honest embrace, the past starts to speak,
Weaving a wisdom for the tender and weak.

Every whisper a promise, a knowing glance,
Inviting the curious to step forth and dance.
With shadows as partners, our doubts cast away,
The truth found within, where darkness won't sway.

In the heart of this book, raw honesty lies,
With each truth revealed, it darkens and sighs.
Shadows whisper softly, where clarity dwells,
In the gentle embrace of the spellbook's spells.

Shades of Imagination in an Ancient Library

In the hushed, sacred hall where the old tales reside,
Shades of imagination in silence abide.
Books lined like soldiers, their stories await,
Whispering colors to the curious fate.

Each spine a portal to lands unexplored,
Where dreams take their flight, and imagination soared.
Time weaves its magic, with history's thread,
Shadows and echoes where thought dares to tread.

Between weathered pages, the past breathes anew,
Ink spills like rivers, in hues that accrue.
Hauntingly beautiful, the whispers take form,
Bright visions igniting, like a gathering storm.

Each glance brings a journey, an adventure to seek,
Words mingling softly, like secrets they speak.
In the ancient library, we gather and share,
Shades of imagination, beyond all compare.

Time drips like honey, sweet and sublime,
In the quiet embrace where all worlds align.
Within these old tomes lies a treasure so vast,
Shades of imagination that gleam from the past.

Enigmatic Phrases Beneath Mystic Stars

Beneath the vast heavens, where whispers entwine,
Enigmatic phrases in starlight do shine.
Each constellation a story to tell,
A tapestry woven where dreams dare to dwell.

In the hush of the night, secrets take flight,
Celestial mysteries in soft, silver light.
Galaxies swirl with a dance of the rare,
Words drift like stardust, suspended in air.

With each twinkle above, a riddle unfolds,
Ethereal languages, both gentle and bold.
In this cosmic embrace, our thoughts intertwine,
Enigmatic phrases that shimmer and shine.

Lost in the wonder, our hearts beat as one,
Tracing the lines of the night's quiet song.
Beneath the great heavens, we dream and we yearn,
Each phrase a reminder, in silence we learn.

In the dance of the stars, a whisper persists,
Beneath mystic shadows, where the universe twists.
With each breath of night, a new story born,
Enigmatic phrases, forever adorned.

Forgotten Epics in a Caster's Realm

In shadows deep, where secrets lie,
Old tales weave like starlit sighs.
A sorcerer's quill, in hand it gleams,
Awakens lost, forgotten dreams.

Echoes of chants from ages past,
Spellbound souls, their fates amassed.
Through mystic tomes with wisdom tight,
The caster's heart ignites the night.

Each rune speaks of battles won,
Of kingdoms lost and battles spun.
With every script, new worlds arise,
Unveiling truths beneath the skies.

A weary heart, yet bold in fight,
Grasps ancient power, claims the light.
With every word, the magic swells,
In every breath, a story tells.

Forgotten realms now breathe anew,
In endless quests, they find their due.
A weave of fate, forever cast,
In the caster's realm, the die is fast.

Mystical Musings of a Wandering Bard

Upon the roads, where tales do bloom,
The wandering bard escapes the gloom.
With lute in hand, beneath the stars,
He sings of love, and laughing scars.

Every town, a tale awaits,
Of twisted fates and open gates.
His voice a breeze, a gentle sway,
In every note, the night turns day.

Whispers of magic in songs he weaves,
In every heart, a spirit believes.
A melody bright, on dreams it floats,
As laughter carries on moonlit boats.

From distant lands to shores unknown,
Each verse he shares, a seed is sown.
A bard's soft words, like morning dew,
Refresh the souls they wander through.

His stories danced on gentle air,
Of gallant knights and maidens fair.
With every string, the past ignites,
Guiding lost hearts through endless nights.

Twirling Whirlwinds of Enchanted Denotation

In a world where words take flight,
Whirlwinds spin through endless night.
They twirl and loop, a lively spree,
Inviting minds to dance and see.

Each syllable, a spell's embrace,
In spirals of time and space.
A twist of fate, a breath of lore,
Whispers echo forevermore.

With every turn, new visions bloom,
Creating worlds that sweep the gloom.
In vibrant hues, the letters swirl,
As thoughts ignite, and dreams unfurl.

Twirling tales with potent charm,
In every sentence, a silken balm.
Enchanted winds, they twist and sway,
Guiding lost souls along their way.

The denotations dance and gleam,
A tapestry of every dream.
In swirling fables, life takes form,
Within the whirlwinds, hearts grow warm.

Spells Whispered on Gentle Breezes

On breezes soft, where secrets play,
The whispers of spells drift away.
Like feathers tossed on currents free,
They carry hopes through land and sea.

Each gentle breath, a magic sigh,
Kisses the earth and lifts the sky.
In harmony, they weave and flow,
The spells of love that softly grow.

From forest glades to mountain high,
The murmurs echo, never shy.
In twilight's warmth, they find their tune,
Beneath the silver light of moon.

With every gust, a promise swells,
The heart's deep song, the spirit yells.
Dreams carried forth on whispers' wings,
Painting life with magical things.

So heed the whispers, pure and bright,
In gentle breezes, find your light.
For every spell that slips away,
Is waiting there for you to say.

Enchanted Sylphs Dancing on Words

In twilight's grace, they weave so bright,
Sylphs twirl softly, in pure delight.
Whispers of ink upon a page,
Their laughter dances, free from cage.

With every turn, a spell they cast,
In rhythm, where the shadows dance.
Letters twinkle, stars in flight,
A tapestry spun, pure and light.

Each syllable a gentle breeze,
Melodies drift, hearts find their ease.
In vibrant hues, their colors bloom,
A garden flourished from every room.

They leap in joy, through phrases wide,
In liquid grace, they do abide.
The magic swells, on verses sweet,
As words collide, and hearts entreat.

Thus, the sylphs, in flight, will stay,
Dancing through the night and day.
Boundless freedom in every line,
In this enchanted world, we'll shine.

The Elegance of Spellbound Poetry

In whispers soft, the verses flow,
An elegant dance, a tender glow.
With every word, a spell is cast,
Capturing moments, a timeless blast.

Pages flutter, like wings in flight,
A symphony born from day and night.
The ink flows deep, like rivers wide,
In echoes of heart, where dreams reside.

Each stanza blooms, a flower's grace,
In gardens rich, they find their place.
The rhythm sings, a gentle tune,
Beneath the watchful, silvery moon.

Within the lines, the magic swells,
A story told, where wonder dwells.
With every breath, our spirits rise,
Entranced by whispers, we touch the skies.

Thus poetry sways, a timeless art,
Binding us close, heart to heart.
In its embrace, we find our way,
Through elegance, night turns to day.

Vanishing Verses of a Dreamweaver

In realms where dreams and shadows play,
The dreamweaver spins, night into day.
Verses scatter like morning mist,
Etched in silence, too quick to twist.

With fleeting words, the visions dance,
In twilight's hold, a stolen chance.
Whispers echo in moonbeam light,
Traces fading, out of sight.

Each thread unraveled, tenderly spun,
Stories linger; yet, they're undone.
A tapestry woven through time's embrace,
In every breath, we find their trace.

Beneath the stars, they softly gleam,
Vanishing lines from a half-formed dream.
In distant realms, their echoes fly,
Like fireflies flitting in the sky.

As dawn approaches, they dissipate,
Leaving behind a yearning state.
Yet in our hearts, they ever stay,
These verses lost, but not astray.

Intricate Runes in Celestial Patterns

In night's embrace, runes softly glow,
Patterns etched in the cosmic flow.
Each symbol whispers secrets past,
In celestial ink, forever cast.

With starlit grace, the signs entwine,
A dance of fate, divine design.
Galaxies swirl in vibrant hues,
Where ancient lore shares hidden views.

In shadows cast, the glyphs align,
Mapping journeys through space and time.
Each stroke a heartbeat, a mortal sigh,
Written in silence, where dreams may fly.

The universe breathes through ancient art,
Awakening souls, stirring the heart.
Intricate runes in patterns blend,
A story unfolding with no end.

Thus we dance, under starlit skies,
In the vibrant pulse where magic lies.
With every breath, the cosmos calls,
Intricate runes within us all.

Whispers Entwined in Mystic Threads

In shadows deep, where secrets dwell,
A whispered tale begins to swell.
Threads of fate, in silence spun,
A journey starts with day's undoing.

Crimson skies with twilight blend,
Hearts in silence dare to mend.
Mystic knots, a tapestry,
Woven dreams of what could be.

Through ancient woods, we softly tread,
Guided by the words unsaid.
In the dark, our spirits soar,
Entwined forever, evermore.

Stars alight like whispers rare,
Breath of night fills the air.
A dance of shadows, light a spark,
Eclipses fade, igniting dark.

With each pulse, my heart aligned,
The essence felt, the truth defined.
In mystic threads, our stories blend,
An everlasting bond, no end.

Enchanted Echoes Beneath the Moon

Beneath the moon, where soft winds sigh,
Enchanting echoes rise and fly.
A lullaby of silver light,
Calls the stars to dance at night.

In the stillness, secrets breathe,
Whispers carried on the leaves.
As shadows weave a gentle cloak,
Hearts embrace the words unspoke.

With every note, a memory glows,
Painting dreams as night bestows.
Echoes linger, softly fade,
In the silence, love is laid.

In twilight's grace, our souls unite,
Bathed in warmth of lunar light.
Threads of time entwined in gold,
Stories whispered, ages old.

Forever caught in moon's embrace,
The night a mirror, time and space.
In enchanted echoes, we remain,
Bound forever, love's refrain.

Spellbound Verses in Feathered Pages

Pages flutter like a winged sigh,
Spellbound verses float and fly.
Ink of dreams on parchment laid,
Captured whispers that won't fade.

Each word a note in melody,
Notes that dance in harmony.
Feathered tips on thoughts we weave,
In every line, a world to leave.

Through every tale, our spirits roam,
Words our compass, page our home.
In sacred silence, stories dwell,
Magic woven with each spell.

As dusk unfolds, our visions soar,
In ink and whispers, we explore.
The feather bright, a guiding muse,
For every heart that dares to choose.

Boundless realms in pages lie,
Breath of wonder as dreams fly.
Spellbound verses, never part,
Treasured moments held in heart.

Woven Secrets of a Sorcerer's Quill

In twilight's grasp, a quill takes flight,
Woven secrets in the night.
With ink like shadows, stories flow,
From whispered dreams that softly glow.

Each stroke a spell, each line a charm,
Crafting worlds with gentle calm.
A sorcerer's hand, deft and sly,
Unveils the truths that never die.

In every word, a heartbeat beats,
Magic lingers where sorcery meets.
Unraveled tales, a timeless quest,
Within the pages, dreams find rest.

Through enchanted ink, we draw the light,
Guiding lost souls through the night.
In woven threads, the past aligns,
With every quill, new fate designs.

As echoes hum in ancient woods,
Woven secrets, understood.
With a flick of wrist, the story spins,
And in each heart, the magic begins.

Gossamer Dreams in the Alchemist's Studio

In the quiet glow of twilight's cheer,
Flasks and vials whisper secrets near.
Golden dust dances in the light,
Merging shadows with ethereal flight.

Potent herbs marinate in jars,
Veils of mystery, like distant stars.
Sparks of wonder ignite the air,
Heartbeats echo with hopeful flair.

Gossamer wings flutter and glide,
Through the studio where dreams reside.
Elixirs bubble, revealing fate,
In every drop, love and hate.

Crimson tinctures in bottles align,
Promises shimmer, their gleams entwine.
A whispered wish escapes the night,
As the alchemist chases the light.

Silver moons glance from high above,
Weaving tales of the heart's true love.
In this realm where time stands still,
Imagination bends to will.

Tangles of Light in a Caster's Grasp

Within the circle, bright orbs collide,
Fingers weaving, worlds coincide.
Threads of light, like fragile threads,
Binding realms where shadows treads.

Chants of power ripple through space,
Casting spells with a dancer's grace.
Colors leap and shimmer bright,
Painting dreams in the starlit night.

The caster smiles, lost in the glow,
Mysteries unfold in their flow.
Every twist ignites a star,
Drawing magic from near and far.

Each pulse and flick, a story unfolds,
In the heart of light, the truth beholds.
With each enchantment, worlds intertwine,
In tangles of fate, both yours and mine.

Delicate Phrasing from the Arcane Ruins

Amidst the stones where whispers breathe,
Phrasings linger amidst the wreath.
Echoes of ancient secrets call,
In the silence, I hear them all.

Winds of fate through crumbling walls,
Carry the magic as twilight falls.
Illuminated glyphs glow faint,
Each curve tells tales both proud and quaint.

A scholar kneels, quill poised to write,
Dancing shadows in the fading light.
Words connect like threads so fine,
Unraveling spells through the design.

In arches high, the past entwined,
Secrets waiting, so well-defined.
With delicate phrasing, time bends near,
Awakening echoes, soft yet clear.

Threads of Twilight in a Grimoire's Dust

Beneath the cover, secrets sleep,
In a grimoire's dust, wisdom deep.
Threads of twilight weave their way,
Through pages worn, where shadows play.

A flickering candle casts soft hues,
Illuminating the forgotten views.
Each line a journey of mystic lore,
Leading the heart to ancient shores.

Whispers of magic, lost in time,
Resting within each verse and rhyme.
A flick of the wrist, a gentle touch,
Summons the past, it means so much.

In silent corners, stories unfurl,
As the night wraps 'round like a pearl.
Threads of twilight gently entwine,
Guiding the seeker through the divine.

The Conjurer's Delicate Lexicon

With whispers soft, the words take flight,
A dance of spells beneath the night.
Each syllable, a thread of fate,
Weaving tales that resonate.

In shadows deep, the secrets dwell,
With every charm, the echoes swell.
A language drawn from ancient lore,
Unlocking doors, forevermore.

The ink runs wild on parchment skin,
A map to worlds yet to begin.
In every verse, a spark ignites,
The flame of magic, pure delights.

To conjure dreams, to shape the light,
In whispered tones, the spirits write.
A delicate lexicon bestowed,
In words of power, truth is sowed.

So let the mind and heart combine,
With every written word, we shine.
The conjurer's art, a sacred muse,
In rhymes and rhythms, we shall choose.

Ethereal Stitches in Rhyme

Beneath the stars, the fabric glows,
With threads of silver, time bestows.
Each line, a stitch in mystic seams,
We craft the essence of our dreams.

The twilight whispers stories old,
In colors bright, their truths unfold.
Through gentle hues, the echoes weave,
A tapestry we all believe.

In verses soft, the shadows dance,
With every beat, a tender glance.
Ethereal stitches, swift and light,
We sew the secrets of the night.

With hands outstretched to catch the glow,
In rhythmic flow, our spirits grow.
Through silent songs, the heart takes flight,
In ethereal stitches, pure delight.

So let the needle guide our fate,
Each rhyme a bond we cultivate.
In this embrace, we merge as one,
With every stitch, our journey's begun.

Sorcery Draped in Gossamer Hues

In twilight's veil, the magic brews,
A world aglow in gossamer hues.
With tendrils light, the spells entwine,
In whispered breaths, the stars align.

With fleeting hands, we shape the air,
Creating dreams with tender care.
Each flick of wand, a shimmer bright,
Draped in wonder, pure delight.

The shadows dance in moonlit beams,
Unraveling the heart's deep dreams.
In tangled webs of night's embrace,
We find a way to know our place.

Through every breath, the magic sings,
In graceful arcs, the sorcery swings.
A tapestry of dreams unfold,
In gossamer threads, a story told.

So let us weave with hope and grace,
A glimpse into the infinite space.
In magic's sway, our souls will fuse,
In sorcery draped in gossamer hues.

Enigmatic Ink on Mystical Pages

In realms where time and space collide,
The ink reveals the fears we hide.
On mystical pages, truths remain,
A dance of thought through joy and pain.

Each stroke a path to worlds unknown,
In portraits drawn where shadows've grown.
With enigmatic flair, we write,
The tales that shimmer in the night.

The quill like wand, in silence glides,
Through every line, the spirit bides.
In whispered spells, the heart expands,
As ink entwines with magic hands.

A canvas rich in dreams untold,
In every word, a spark unfolds.
The stories linger, wild and free,
Enigmatic ink, our legacy.

So let us write till dawn has come,
In mysteries, our hearts succumb.
On mystical pages, we'll engage,
With enigmatic ink, we craft the sage.

Celestial Scribe of the Midnight Realm

Beneath the stars, where shadows creep,
The scribe weaves tales from dreams of sleep.
Ink spills bright, a cosmic dance,
Each word a wish, a fleeting chance.

Time drips slow in lunar light,
Whispers echo through the night.
Pages flutter, secrets shared,
In the dark, his heart laid bare.

Galaxies swirl in ink's embrace,
He captures worlds with quiet grace.
Mysteries hum in every line,
Stories pulse, like stars, they shine.

Veils of night unveil the truth,
A sacred bond of timeless youth.
Beyond the veil, where shadows play,
The scribe's quill carves night to day.

With every stroke, the cosmos spin,
A tale unfolds, where dreams begin.
Through the silence, his voice rings clear,
The cosmos listens, drawn near.

Velvet Incantations in the Silent Library

Within the hush of velvet nights,
Whispers dwell in hidden sights.
Pages turn, the softest sigh,
Magic lingers as time slips by.

Candles flicker with golden gleams,
A world awakes, alive with dreams.
Each row holds a story untold,
Secrets shimmer in silence bold.

Ink spells cast on parchment fine,
Words intertwine, a soft divine.
Echoes breathe through every shelf,
History rests in timeless self.

Crimson binds and leathered tomes,
Ancient whispers feel like home.
With gentle hands, the night unfolds,
Velvet magic, a heart that holds.

Through silent halls, enchantments weave,
A tapestry of tales we leave.
Lifetimes linger in every stare,
In this realm, worries disappear.

Charmed Sonnets on the Apprentice's Desk

In the soft glow of a candle's flame,
An apprentice dreams, pursues the aim.
Parchment waits with eager grace,
For sonnets born in a sacred space.

Feathered quill in trembling hand,
A world awaits at his command.
Words like spells, they twist and twine,
In every line, a spark divine.

Rhyme and reason softly blend,
Charmed sonnets gently send.
Each verse a step to realms unknown,
In whispered tones, his heart has grown.

Ink as deep as a midnight sea,
Crafting magic, wild and free.
Echoes of wisdom softly call,
In their embrace, he fears no fall.

Through the night, his thoughts take flight,
Beautiful visions dancing in sight.
A tale unfurls, and dreams ignite,
The apprentice blooms in silver light.

Each sonnet whispered to the stars,
Paints his journey, healing scars.
The desk, alive with fervent dreams,
A keeper of hope, where magic beams.

Luminescent Lines in a Sorcery's Embrace

In the twilight of unfurling night,
Lines of light cascade bright.
Sorcery hums in the air-filled space,
A dance of shadows in a warm embrace.

Chasing whispers through the dark,
Lanterns flicker, igniting spark.
With every stroke, a tale unfolds,
In the realm where magic holds.

Luminescent dreams brush the page,
Awakening thoughts from an ancient sage.
Mystical runes begin to sway,
Guiding hearts along the way.

A sigil drawn in golden ink,
Inviting wonders, daring to think.
In shadows deep, the secrets grow,
As magic turns, the night aglow.

Threads of fate entwined, they bind,
The lines blaze forth, a pure design.
In sorcery's heart, truths ignite,
Transforming whispers into light.

From pen to paper, a spark released,
The world of wonders never ceased.
In this embrace, the soul takes flight,
Luminescent lines in sacred night.